STUDY GUIDE TO ACCOMPANY

PROFESSIONAL

BAKING

Fourth Edition

WAYNE GISSLEN

WILEY
JOHN WILEY & SONS, INC.

Library of Congress Cataloging-in-Publication Data:

ISBN: 0-471-47777-X

Printed in the United States of America.

10 9 8 7

Contents

TO THE STUDENT

This manual is a companion to the fourth edition of *Professional Baking*. Its purpose is to help you study and review the material in the text.

Learning to bake and to prepare pastries and desserts is to a great extent a practical, hands-on endeavor. Much of your training involves learning manual skills by practicing them under the guidance of an instructor or supervisor, and then improving those skills by repeated practice.

These practical skills, however, depend on a large body of knowledge and understanding. You need to know about such essential matters as gluten development, characteristics of various flours and other baking ingredients, measurement, formula structure, and procedures for preparing the basic doughs, batters, creams, and fillings. Using this manual will help you study and master this material.

This study guide is arranged by chapter, corresponding to the 22 chapters in *Professional Baking*. Each chapter contains several exercises that you can use to test your knowledge. This manual will help you see what you have learned and what you need to review. The following are guidelines for using the different kinds of exercises.

CHAPTER GOALS

Chapter goals are repeated from the beginning of each text chapter. They are not exercises, but they are included here as a reminder of the specific skills you should be learning in each chapter.

TERMS

The first exercise in each chapter is a list of definitions or descriptions of terms used in the bakeshop. In each of the blanks provided, write the term that is defined or described.

This is the only kind of exercise you will find in every chapter. Why is there so much emphasis on terms? It is important not only that you learn how to bake but that you can communicate with other bakers and cooks. A food service career involves teamwork and sharing of information. To communicate, you must know the language of the bakeshop and kitchen.

COMPLETION, SHORT-ANSWER QUESTIONS, AND OTHER WRITTEN EXERCISES

Many exercises ask you to fill in blanks with words or phrases or to write out various kinds of answers.

If the problem is a regular question, a space is provided in which you can write out the answer.

If the problem is a statement that contains one or more blanks, fill in the blanks so that the statement is accurate and makes a complete sentence.

If the problem asks you to write a procedure or to explain how to do a task, write out the procedure using numbered steps. You do not need to *explain* each step, the way the text sometimes does, but be sure that your procedure is complete. Don't leave out any steps.

TRUE/FALSE QUESTIONS

For each question, draw a circle around the *T* if the statement is *completely* true. Draw a circle around the *F* if the statement is only *partly* true or is *completely* false.

MATH EXERCISES

Math is very important in the bakeshop and the pastry kitchen. Throughout your career you will have to make many kinds of mathematical calculations. Some of the most basic of these are explained in *Professional Baking*.

Some of the most important calculations you will have to make in the bakeshop involve converting formulas to get different yields. This is done using a system of percentages, as explained in Chapter 1. Calculations involving baker's percentages are included throughout this workbook, to give you practice.

Other kinds of math problems are included in appropriate chapters. Whenever you have difficulty with any of the math problems, turn to the explanation in the text and review it.

These are the kinds of exercises you will find most often in this manual. There are also other kinds of problems and questions that are especially included to help you review the material in a particular chapter. The instructions at the beginning of each of these sections explain how to do the problems.

Chapter 1

Basic Principles

This chapter provides an introduction to bakeshop production. It is important to be very familiar with the information it contains because this chapter lays the foundation for all of your work in the bakeshop. Principles of measurement and formula structure are discussed, as well as the factors that affect development of gluten in various doughs and batters. In addition, you will learn about the changes that take place in a dough or batter as it is baked.

After studying Chapter 1, you should be able to

1. Explain the importance of weighing baking ingredients.
2. Use a baker's balance scale.
3. Use formulas based on baker's percentages.
4. Explain the factors that control the development of gluten in baked products.
5. Explain the changes that take place in a dough or batter as it bakes.
6. Prevent or retard the staling of baked items.

1

A. TERMS

Fill in each blank with the term that is defined or described.

_____ 1. A baker's term for weighing, usually of ingredients or of doughs or batters.

_____ 2. An elastic substance made up of proteins in wheat flour.

_____ 3. The process by which proteins become firm, usually when heated.

_____ 4. Prefix in the metric system meaning "one-hundredth."

_____ 5. Prefix in the metric system meaning "one thousand."

_____ 6. Prefix in the metric system meaning "one-tenth."

_____ 7. The basic unit of length in the metric system; slightly longer than three feet.

_____ 8. Prefix in the metric system meaning "one-thousandth."

_____ 9. Basic unit of volume in the metric system; slightly larger than one quart.

_____ 10. Basic unit of weight in the metric system; equal to about one-thirtieth of an ounce.

_____ 11. The change in texture and aroma of baked goods due to the loss of moisture from the starch granules.

_____ 12. Flour with a high protein content.

_____ 13. Any fat used in baking to tenderize a product by shortening gluten strands.

_____ 14. Flour with a low protein content.

_____ 15. The process by which starch granules absorb water and swell in size.

_____ 16. The gas released by the action of yeast and by baking powder and baking soda.

_____ 17. The production or incorporation of gases, followed by the expansion of these gases, in a baked product, which increases the volume of the product and changes its texture.

_____ 18. The basic unit of temperature in the metric system.

_____ 19. The basic unit of temperature in the U.S. system of measurement.

B. SHORT-ANSWER QUESTIONS

Fill in the blanks as required.

1. What are the four major factors that determine how much gluten will be developed in a dough or batter?

   _____

   _____

   _____

   _____.

2. The most accurate way to measure dry ingredients in the bakeshop is

   _____.

3. A cookie or pastry that is very crumbly due to high _____ content and

   little _____ development is said to be "short."

4. Two factors that cause baked goods to become stale are loss of _____

   and a chemical change in starch structure called: _____

   _____.

5. Loss of crispness is caused by the absorption of _____.

6. List three ways to slow the staling of baked goods.

   _____

   _____

   _____.

7. List the seven stages of the baking process.

_____

_____

_____

_____

_____

_____

_____

C. UNITS OF MEASURE

For each of the following abbreviations, write out the full name of the unit of measure in the space provided.

1. lb   _____

2. ml   _____

3. qt   _____

4. dl   _____

5. oz   _____

6. pt   _____

7. tsp   _____

8. g   _____

9. gal   _____

10. cm   _____

11. kg   _____

12. tbsp _____

13 l _____

14. mm _____

15. cl _____

Fill in the blanks by making the correct conversion.

16. 6 fl oz = _____ tbsp

17. 3 ¾ lb = _____ oz

18. 9 tsp = _____ tbsp

19. 20 oz = _____ lb

20. ½ gal = _____ pt

21. 1 ½ cups = _____ fl oz

22. 2 ½ fl oz = _____ tsp

23. 1 ¾ pt = _____ fl oz

24. 10 tbsp = _____ fl oz

25. 48 fl oz = _____ qt

26. 4 ½ lb = _____ oz

27. 60 oz = _____ lb

28. 0.1 kg = _____ g

29. 2300 ml = _____ l

30. 1.6 kg = _____ g

31. 6 dl = _____ ml

32. 12 cl = _____ ml

33. 1750 g   =   _____ kg

34. 150 ml   =   _____ l

35. 750 g   =   _____ kg

D. USING BAKER'S PERCENTAGES

Use the percentages given to calculate the quantities needed in the following formulas. (You are provided with either the weight of the flour or the total yield by weight.) Fill in the blanks with your answers. Do either the U.S. or Metric calculations or both as indicated by your instructor.

I.

Butter	_____	67%	_____
Sugar	_____	115%	_____
Salt	_____	1.5%	_____
Unsweetened chocolate	_____	33%	_____
Eggs	_____	50%	_____
Cake flour	12 oz	100%	375 g
Baking powder	_____	4%	_____
Milk	_____	50%	_____
Vanilla	_____	2%	_____

II.

Ingredient		Percent	
Water	_____	50%	_____
Yeast	_____	3%	_____
Flour	_____	100%	_____
Malt syrup	_____	6%	_____
Salt	_____	1.5%	_____
Oil	_____	0.5%	_____
Yield	9 lb 10 oz	161%	4425 g

III.

Ingredient		Percent	
Water	_____	40%	_____
Yeast	_____	5%	_____
Shortening	_____	25%	_____
Sugar	_____	20%	_____
Salt	_____	1.25%	_____
Eggs	_____	15%	_____
Bread flour	3 lb 12 oz	75%	1800 g
Cake flour	1 lb 4 oz	25%	600 g

Chapter 2

Baking and Pastry Equipment

Bread baking and pastry making require a great deal of equipment. Some of this equipment is familiar to any cook. Pots, pans, and knives, for example are used in the bakeshop as well as in the kitchen. On the other hand, there is a great deal of specialized equipment that is used primarily in the bakeshop. This chapter provides an introduction to this special equipment, from mixers and deck ovens to baking molds in many shapes. You will not be using all of this equipment at once, but you should have a general idea of the kinds of tools available to you for the many tasks you will need to perform now and in the future.

Because this chapter is devoted entirely to the identification of equipment items and their uses, there is only one section of exercises: Terms.

After studying Chapter 2, you should be able to

Identify the principal equipment used in baking and pastry making and indicate their uses.

A. TERMS

Fill in each blank with the term that is defined or described.

_____	1.	A mixer with a removable bowl and a beater attachment that spins around its own axis while at the same time revolving in an orbit to reach all parts of the bowl.
_____	2.	A machine that cuts a "press" of dough into smaller, equal-size pieces.
_____	3.	A covered loaf pan for baking bread that yields square slices.
_____	4.	A stainless steel ring used for making molded desserts and for shaping and holding desserts made up of layers of cake, pastry, and fillings.
_____	5.	A small, boat-shaped mold.
_____	6.	A dome-shaped mold for frozen desserts.
_____	7.	A mixer with a spiral beater attachment and a rotating bowl.
_____	8.	A machine that cuts a "press" of dough into equal portions and then shapes each portion into a ball.
_____	9.	A machine that rolls dough into sheets by means of rollers and a conveyor belt.
_____	10.	An oven in which breads and other goods are baked directly on the floor of the oven.
_____	11.	A type of refrigerator that maintains a high humidity to prevent doughs from drying.
_____	12.	A bentwood basket used for proofing loaves of bread.
_____	13.	A stainless steel pan for holding foods in service counters; also used for baking and steaming items such as bread pudding.

_____ 14. A ring-shaped or doughnut-shaped mold for baking a yeast item of the same name.

_____ 15. A cake pan with a removable bottom.

_____ 16. A deep pan with a tube in the center, used mainly for baking angel food cakes.

_____ 17. A baking pan with shell-shaped indentations, used for baking small cakes of the same name.

_____ 18. A tool, consisting of a handle attached to a rotating tube fitted with spikes, for piercing holes in rolled-out dough.

_____ 19. A thin, flat board with a long handle, used for inserting and removing hearth breads from ovens.

_____ 20. A tool for measuring the density of syrups.

_____ 21. A mixer attachment used for mixing and kneading yeast doughs.

_____ 22. A machine that rolls and forms pieces of bread dough for standard loaves, baguettes, and rolls.

_____ 23. A box used to create the ideal temperature and humidity for fermenting yeast products.

_____ 24. A large oven into which entire racks of sheet pans can be wheeled.

_____ 25. A steam kettle that can be tilted.

_____ 26. A small plastic tool, usually triangular, with edges cut in different patterns, used for decorating or texturing icings.

_____ 27. A round, flat disk that swivels freely on a pedestal; used for holding cakes for decorating.

_____ 28. A sheet of heavy linen or canvas, used for holding certain types of breads, such as baguettes, as they are proofed.

Chapter 3

Ingredients

A baker must be thoroughly familiar with the basic ingredients of the bakeshop in order to handle them properly in production. This chapter introduces you to the most important characteristics of these ingredients. Special emphasis is on the properties of various flours, which are of course the baker's primary ingredients.

After studying Chapter 3, you should be able to

1. Understand the characteristics and functions of the major baking ingredients.
2. Make appropriate adjustments in formulas when substituting ingredients, such as dry milk for liquid milk and dry yeast for cake yeast.
3. Identify the main types of wheat flours by sight and feel.

A. TERMS

Fill in each blank with the term that is defined or described.

_____ 1. Any of a group of solid fats, usually white and tasteless, that have been specially formulated for baking.

_____ 2. The chemical name for regular granulated sugar and confectioners' sugar.

_____ 3. The process of beating fat and sugar together to incorporate air.

_____ 4. A mixture of solid fats and other substances intended to resemble butter.

_____ 5. Flour made from the entire wheat kernel minus the bran and germ.

_____ 6. A mixture of two simple sugars, dextrose and levulose, resulting from the breakdown of sucrose.

_____ 7. A heavy brown syrup made from sugar cane.

_____ 8. The process of whipping eggs, sometimes with sugar, to incorporate air.

_____ 9. A flavoring ingredient consisting of flavorful oils and other substances dissolved in alcohol.

_____ 10. Flour from soft wheat with a low protein content.

_____ 11. Flour from hard wheat with a high protein content.

_____ 12. A dark, coarse meal or flour made from entire rye grains.

_____ 13. A tan-colored wheat flour made from the outer portion of the endosperm.

_____ 14. The process by which yeast changes sugars into alcohol and carbon dioxide gas.

_____ 15. The hard outer covering of kernels of wheat and other grains.

_____ 16. The plant embryo portion of a grain kernel.

_____ 17. A type of syrup, extracted from malted barley, containing maltose sugar.

_____ 18. The production or incorporation of gases in a baked product to increase volume and produce shape and texture.

_____ 19. The product that results when cocoa beans are roasted and ground.

_____ 20. The whitish or yellowish fat that is a natural component of cocoa beans.

_____ 21. The finest or smoothest variety of confectioners' sugar.

_____ 22. The starchy inner portion of grain kernels.

_____ 23. The percentage of a grain kernel that is separated into a particular grade of flour.

_____ 24. Various enzymes, found in flour and in some malts, that convert starch into sugar.

_____ 25. A fine quality of wheat flour that is milled from the inner portions of the endosperm.

_____ 26. A weak flour with a soft, smooth texture and a pure white color.

_____ 27. Wheat flour to which bran flakes have been added.

_____ 28. A mixture of rye flour and strong wheat flour.

_____ 29. Cocoa that has been processed with an alkali.

_____ 30. A mixture of finely ground almonds and sugar.

_____ 31. A soft shortening with special additives that enable the shortening to be blended with larger quantities of sugar and liquid than regular shortenings can.

_____ 32. The dry powder that results when natural fats are separated from roasted, ground cocoa beans.

_____ 33. A water-soluble protein extracted from animal tissue, used as a jelling agent.

_____ 34. A water-soluble plant fiber used as a jelling agent.

_____ 35. A simple sugar available in the form of a clear, colorless, tasteless syrup.

_____ 36. French term used for high-quality natural sweetened chocolate, containing no added fats other than cocoa butter.

_____ 37. A slightly aged, cultured heavy cream.

_____ 38. The mineral content of flour.

_____ 39. The amount of water that a given flour can take up to form a dough of a standard consistency, expressed as a percentage of the weight of the flour.

B. FLOUR REVIEW

Briefly describe, using your own words, the *break system* for milling flour. Explain the term *extraction* as it relates to milling different grades of flour.

_____

_____

_____

_____

_____

_____

Since flour is the most important ingredient in the bakeshop, familiarity with different types of flour is necessary. Define or describe each of the following products. If the product is a wheat flour, indicate whether it is a strong or weak flour.

1. Straight flour: _____

_____

_____.

2. Patent flour: _____

_____

_____.

3. Bread flour: _____

_____

_____.

4. Clear flour: _____

_____

_____.

5. Cake flour: _____

_____

_____.

6. Pastry flour: _____

_____

_____.

7. Whole wheat flour: _____

_____

_____.

8. Bran flour: _____

_____

_____.

9. Rye flour: _____

_____

_____.

10. Rye meal: _____

_____

_____.

11. Rye blend: _____

_____

_____.

C. SHORT-ANSWER QUESTIONS

1. List five functions of fats in baked goods.

(a) _____.

(b) _____.

(c) _____.

(d) _____.

(e) _____.

2. Why are pastry doughs made with butter often more difficult to handle than those made with shortening? _____

   _____

   _____

   _____.

3. What are two advantages of using butter instead of shortening in a pastry dough?

   _____

   _____.

4. List eight functions of eggs in baked products.

   (a) _____.

   (b) _____.

   (c) _____.

   (d) _____.

   (e) _____,

   (f) _____.

   (g) _____.

   (h) _____.

5. Describe two ways of incorporating air into batters to provide leavening.

    (a) _____

    _____.

    (b) _____.

    _____.

6. At what temperatures does yeast grow best? _____.

    At what temperature is yeast killed? _____.

7. What are three functions of salt in baked goods?

    (a) _____.

    (b) _____.

    (c) _____.

8. Why does devil's food cake have a reddish color? _____

    _____.

9. Describe, in three general steps, how unflavored gelatin is incorporated into a recipe.

    _____

    _____

    _____

D. BAKESHOP MATH (U.S. Measures)

1. A formula for biscuits requires 1 lb 8 oz skim milk and is leavened with 2 oz baking powder. A baker wishes to substitute buttermilk for the skim milk. How should the leavening be adjusted to compensate for the buttermilk? (Give exact quantities.)

    _____

    _____

2. A formula for muffins requires 6 pints skim milk and is leavened with 7 oz baking powder. A baker wishes to substitute buttermilk for the skim milk. How should the leavening be adjusted to compensate for the buttermilk? (Give exact quantities.)

    _____

    _____ .

3. A quick bread recipe requires 2 lb buttermilk and is leavened with 1.25 oz baking soda. A baker wishes to substitute skim milk for the buttermilk.

    How should the leavening be adjusted? _____

    _____ .

4. A formula requires 1 lb 12 oz bitter (unsweetened) chocolate and 2 lb 8 oz shortening. A baker wishes to substitute natural cocoa powder for the chocolate.

    How much cocoa should be used? _____ .

    How much shortening should be used? _____ .

5. A formula requires 12 oz cocoa powder and 1 lb 4 oz shortening. A baker wishes to substitute unsweetened chocolate for the cocoa.

    How much chocolate should be used? _____ .

    How much shortening should be used? _____ .

E.   BAKESHOP MATH (Metric Measures)

1.   A formula for biscuits requires 750 g skim milk and is leavened with 60 g baking powder. A baker wishes to substitute buttermilk for the skim milk. How should the leavening be adjusted to compensate for the buttermilk? (Give exact quantities.)

_____

_____

2.   A formula for muffins requires 3 L skim milk and is leavened with 210 g baking powder. A baker wishes to substitute buttermilk for the skim milk. How should the leavening be adjusted to compensate for the buttermilk? (Give exact quantities.)

_____

_____.

3.   A quick bread recipe requires 1 kg buttermilk and is leavened with 40 g baking soda. A baker wishes to substitute skim milk for the buttermilk.

How should the leavening be adjusted? _____

_____.

4.   A formula requires 850 g bitter (unsweetened) chocolate and 1200 g shortening. A baker wishes to substitute natural cocoa powder for the chocolate.

How much cocoa should be used? _____.

How much shortening should be used? _____.

5.   A formula requires 350 g cocoa powder and 580 g shortening. A baker wishes to substitute unsweetened chocolate for the cocoa.

How much chocolate should be used? _____.

How much shortening should be used? _____.

Chapter 4

Understanding Yeast Doughs

Breads and other yeast goods are perhaps the most important products of the bakeshop. Breads are a large area of study, so we have divided the subject matter into four chapters. This chapter discusses procedures for making breads and other yeast products. Special emphasis is placed on various types of dough-making processes and on controlling fermentation. Chapter 5 introduces more advanced subject matter related to artisan breads. Specific formulas and makeup techniques are included in Chapters 6 and 7.

After studying Chapter 4, you should be able to

1. List and describe the twelve basic steps in the production of yeast goods.
2. Explain the three basic mixing methods used for yeast doughs.
3. Understand and control the factors affecting dough fermentation.
4. Recognize and correct faults in yeast products.

A. TERMS

Fill in each blank with the term that is defined or described.

_____ 1. A method of deflating dough to expel carbon dioxide.

_____ 2. A dough that is low in fat and sugar.

_____ 3. A dough that is high in fat, sugar, and sometimes eggs.

_____ 4. The rapid rise of a yeast dough in the oven due to the production and expansion of gases.

_____ 5. The process by which yeast acts on carbohydrates to produce alcohol and carbon dioxide.

_____ 6. A dough that has not fermented long enough.

_____ 7. Refrigerating a yeast dough to slow the fermentation.

_____ 8. A bread dough that is made with a large quantity of yeast and given no fermentation time except for a short rest after mixing.

_____ 9. The process of shaping scaled dough into smooth, round balls.

_____ 10. A dough in which fat is incorporated into the dough in many layers by using a folding and rolling procedure.

_____ 11. A liquid that is brushed onto the surface of a product, usually before baking.

_____ 12. A bread that is baked directly on the bottom of the oven, not in a pan.

_____ 13. A yeast dough mixing method in which all ingredients are combined at once.

_____ 14. A yeast dough mixing method in which flour and other ingredients are mixed into a yeast batter or dough that has already had some fermentation time.

_____ 15. The continuation of the yeast action, as described in number 6, after the dough has been shaped into loaves or other products, resulting in increase in volume.

_____ 16. A machine that can be set to retard dough and then automatically to begin proofing the dough at a preset time.

B. TRUE OR FALSE

T   F   1. Hard-crusted breads, such as French bread, should not be wrapped.

T   F   2. Hard-crusted breads, such as French bread, should not be refrigerated.

T   F   3. High butter content in a yeast dough encourages more rapid fermentation.

T   F   4. Overmixing is never a problem with lean bread doughs because of their strong gluten content.

T   F   5. Baking with steam helps to form a thick crust on French bread.

T   F   6. Dinner rolls should be proofed at about 75° F.

T   F   7. Low humidity should be used for proofing hard rolls to keep them from forming soggy crusts.

T   F   8.   Hearth breads are baked with the seams on the bottom.

T   F   9.   Salt weakens gluten.

T   F   10.   Lean doughs usually require longer proofing than rich doughs.

C. YEAST DOUGH PRODUCTION

1.   List the twelve steps in the production of yeast goods.

    1.   _____

    2.   _____

    3.   _____

    4.   _____

    5.   _____

    6.   _____

    7.   _____

    8.   _____

    9.   _____

  10.   _____

  11.   _____

  12.   _____

2. In the space below, write the procedure for mixing yeast doughs by the straight dough method.

3. In the space below, write the procedure for mixing yeast doughs by the modified straight dough method. For what types of doughs is this method used? Why?

4.   In the space below, write the procedure for mixing yeast doughs by the sponge method.

D. BAKESHOP MATH (U.S. Measures)

1. A formula requiring 8 ounces of yeast has a fermentation time of 90 minutes at 80° F. How much yeast is required if the baker wishes to increase the fermentation time to 2 hours?

    _____.

2. A formula requiring 1 pound of yeast has a fermentation time of 2 hours at 80° F. How much yeast is required if the baker wishes to reduce the fermentation time to 90 minutes?

    _____.

3. Given the following, factors, calculate the water temperature needed to make a mixed dough with a temperature of 80° F.

Flour temperature	=	74° F
Room temperature	=	75° F
Machine friction	=	20° F

    Water temperature = _____

4. Given the following factors, calculate the water temperature needed to make a mixed dough with a temperature of 75° F.

Flour temperature	=	70° F
Room temperature	=	73° F
Machine friction	=	20° F

    Water temperature = _____

E.   BAKESHOP MATH (Metric Measures)

1.   A formula requiring 250 g yeast has a fermentation time of 90 minutes at 27° C. How much yeast is required if the baker wishes to increase the fermentation time to 2 hours?

   _____.

2.   A formula requiring 450 g yeast has a fermentation time of 2 hours at 27° C. How much yeast is required if the baker wishes to reduce the fermentation time to 90 minutes?

   _____.

3.   Given the following, factors, calculate the water temperature needed to make a mixed dough with a temperature of 26° C.

   Flour temperature   =   23° C
   Room temperature   =   24° C
   Machine friction   =   11° C

   Water temperature   =   _____

4.   Given the following factors, calculate the water temperature needed to make a mixed dough with a temperature of 24° C.

   Flour temperature   =   21° C
   Room temperature   =   23° C
   Machine friction   =   11° C

   Water temperature   =   _____

Chapter 5

Understanding Artisan Breads

Breads and other yeast goods are perhaps the most important products of the bakeshop. Breads are a large area of study, so we have divided the subject matter into two chapters. This chapter discusses procedures for making breads and other yeast products. Special emphasis is placed on various types of dough-making processes and on controlling fermentation. Specific formulas and makeup techniques are included in Chapters 4 and 5.

After studying Chapter 5, you should be able to

1. Select flour for making artisan breads.
2. Prepare yeast pre-ferments.
3. Prepare and maintain a sourdough starter.
4. Mix bread doughs using the technique called *autolyse*.
5. Bake artisan breads properly.

A. TERMS

Fill in each blank with the term that is defined or described.

_____ 1. A handmade bread made according to traditional methods, without chemical additives, and with pre-ferments.

_____ 2. French term for sourdough starter.

_____ 3. The type of bacteria most common in sourdough starters.

_____ 4. A yeast pre-ferment made of equal weights of flour and water.

_____ 5. Italian term for a stiff yeast pre-ferment.

_____ 6. The process of hydrating flour before mixing with yeast and salt.

_____ 7. French term for yeast pre-ferment.

_____ 8. A dough leavened by a sourdough starter.

_____ 9. A fermented dough that is used to leaven a larger batch of dough.

_____ 10. French term for yeast.

_____ 11. A thin or wet sourdough starter.

_____ 12. French term for scrap dough.

B. TRUE OR FALSE

T   F   1.   Biga and poolish are two types of yeast pre-ferment.

T   F   2.   Most breads referred to as "artisan" are hearth breads.

T   F   3.   Barm and pâte fermentée are two types of sourdough starter.

T   F   4.   In order to be called "artisan," a bread must contain no ingredients other than flour, water, salt, and yeast.

T   F   5.   The purpose of autolyse is to give the yeast a head start so that fermentation will be faster.

T   F   6.   Artisan breads are generally fermented at a lower temperature than typical commercially made breads.

T   F   7.   European-style breads use stronger flours than typical North American breads.

T   F   8.   High-extraction flour usually is darker in color than patent flour.

T   F   9.   Mixed fermentation refers to the use of both a pre-ferment and additional yeast to ferment a dough.

T   F   10.   A thin or wet sourdough starter is more stable than a stiff, dough-like starter.

C. SOURDOUGH PRODUCTION

In the space below, write the procedure for making a sourdough starter.

Chapter 6

Lean Yeast Doughs

The general procedures and theories discussed in Chapter 4 and 5 are applied to specific formulas and makeup techniques for lean dough products in Chapter 6. As you mix, shape, pan, and bake the products in this chapter, review the explanations and procedures in Chapter 4 and 5 as necessary.

After studying Chapter 6, you should be able to

1. Prepare lean straight doughs and sponge doughs.
2. Prepare natural starters and starters, and mix sourdoughs using them.
3. Make up a variety of loaf and roll types using lean doughs.
4. Prepare a variety of specialty bread items with nonstandard makeup and baking techniques, including English muffins, crumpets, and bagels.

A. TERMS

Fill in each blank with the term that is defined or described.

_____ 1. A coarse, heavy bread made with rye meal.

_____ 2. A rectangular loaf made in a pan with a lid.

_____ 3. A yeast dough made with a sponge or starter that has fermented so long that it has become very acidic or sour.

_____ 4. A scaled unit of dough to be put into a dough divider.

_____ 5. A French regional bread made in the shape of a trellis or ladder.

_____ 6. A French regional bread made in the shape of a trellis or ladder.

_____ 7. A disk-shaped yeast product made from a soft dough and cooked on a griddle.

_____ 8. A disk-shaped yeast product made from a batter and cooked in a metal ring on a griddle.

_____ 9. A type of Italian yeast bread made from a slack dough deposited on pans with minimal shaping.

_____ 10. An Italian flat bread similar to a thick pizza dough.

_____ 11. French name for country-style bread.

B. TRUE OR FALSE

T	F	1.	French breads always contain shortening, while the fat used in Italian bread is olive oil.
T	F	2.	French bread is given a very short proof in order to create the characteristic dense texture.
T	F	3.	Bagels are boiled before baking.
T	F	4.	Sour doughs are somewhat difficult to handle because they are generally stickier than regular bread doughs.
T	F	5.	One standard press makes 25 rolls.
T	F	6.	Ciabatta is made with a stiff dough.
T	F	7.	Yeast starters take longer to develop than natural starters.
T	F	8.	Sour starters are maintained by adding more flour and water to them each day in the same proportion as the original formula.
T	F	9.	Sourdoughs containing a high proportion of sour are usually underproofed.
T	F	10.	Soft pretzels are dipped in a baking soda solution before being baked.

C.   USING BAKER'S PERCENTAGES

Use the percentages given to calculate the quantities needed in the following formulas. (You are provided with either the weight of the flour or the total yield by weight.) Fill in the blanks with your answers. Do either the U.S. or Metric calculations or both as indicated by your instructor.

I.

Water	_____	62%	_____
Yeast, fresh	_____	4%	_____
Bread flour	4 lb	100%	2000 g
Salt	_____	2%	_____
Sugar	_____	4%	_____

II.

Bread flour	_____	100%	_____
Sugar	_____	10%	_____
Salt	_____	2%	_____
Yeast, fresh	_____	3%	_____
Eggs	_____	10%	_____
Milk	_____	50%	_____
Butter	_____	15%	_____
Malt syrup	_____	1%	_____
Yield	7 lb	191%	3400 g

Chapter 7

Rich Yeast Doughs

Just as in Chapter 6, the formulas and makeup techniques presented in this chapter are based on the general theories and procedures explained in Chapter 4. Review the procedures in Chapter 4 as necessary to enable you to make the doughs and perform the makeup techniques in this chapter.

Pay special attention to the rolling-in procedure for Danish and croissant doughs. This is an important technique to master. You will find that careful practice of this procedure in this section will help you when you come to the slightly different rolling-in procedure for puff pastry, as explained in Chapter 12.

After studying chapter 7, you should be able to:

1. Produce simple sweet doughs.
2. Produce rolled–in yeast doughs.
3. Produce a variety of toppings and fillings for rich yeast doughs.
4. Make up a variety of products using sweet doughs and rolled–in doughs, including Danish pastry and croissants.

A. TERMS

Fill in each blank with the term that is defined or described.

_____   1.   Crumb topping for pastries, made of flour, butter, and sugar.

_____   2.   A crescent-shaped roll made with a rolled-in dough.

_____   3.   A dough in which fat is incorporated into the dough in many layers by using a folding and rolling procedure.

_____   4.   Another name for a type of sweet almond filling.

_____   5.   French name for a type of rich, flaky roll with a chocolate filling.

_____   6.   A fold used to make Danish dough, in which the dough is folded in thirds.

_____   7.   A rich yeast dough containing large amounts of eggs and butter, usually made into rolls with round topknots and baked in fluted tins.

_____   8.   A type of yeast bread or cake that is soaked in syrup.

_____   9.   An Italian sweet bread made in a large, round loaf, usually containing dried and candied fruits.

B. TRUE OR FALSE

T   F   1.   Because the gluten is not as strong in sweet roll dough as it is in white bread dough, the sweet roll dough is given a fuller proof.

T   F   2.   The sponge method is often used for mixing sweet doughs.

T   F   3.   Croissants and brioche are two examples of rolled-in dough products.

T   F   4.   When a rich dough contains a high proportion of sugar, the sugar is often creamed with the fat so that it will be more evenly distributed in the dough.

T   F   5.   Sheet pans for baking sweet dough products should be greased heavily and not lined with silicone paper, in order to prevent the bottoms from burning.

T   F   6.   A kugelhopf is baked in a buttered tube pan.

T   F   7.   Croissant dough contains more eggs than Danish dough.

T   F   8.   After the butter is enclosed in the dough for Danish dough, the dough is given four simple folds or turns.

T   F   9.   When most sweet dough products are iced with flat icing, the icing is drizzled over them; it doesn't cover them completely.

T   F   10.   Bear claws, Danish spirals, and Danish pockets are all made up from filled dough rolls.

C. USING BAKER'S PERCENTAGES

Use the percentages given to calculate the quantities needed in the following formulas. (You are provided with either the weight of the flour or the total yield by weight.) Fill in the blanks with your answers. Do either the U.S. or Metric calculations or both as indicated by your instructor.

I.

Milk	_____	30%	_____
Yeast, fresh	_____	5%	_____
Bread flour	_____	33%	_____
Butter	_____	40%	_____
Sugar	_____	20%	_____
Salt	_____	1.25%	_____
Eggs	_____	37%	_____
Bread flour	_____	67%	_____
Raisins	_____	10%	_____
Yield	<u>4 lb 8 oz</u>	243%	<u>2190 g</u>

II.

Milk		16%	
Yeast, fresh		5%	
Bread flour	10 oz	20%	300 g

Eggs		54%	
Bread flour	2 lb 8 oz	80%	1200 g
Sugar		5%	
Salt		1.25%	
Butter		70%	

Chapter 8

Quick Breads

Although this chapter is short, it explains some important procedures that are used to prepare a variety of popular baked goods. These products also have the advantage of being relatively quick and easy to prepare.

After studying Chapter 8, you should be able to

1. Prepare baking powder biscuits and variations of them.
2. Prepare muffins, quick loaf breads, coffee cakes, and corn breads.
3. Prepare popovers.

A.   TERMS

Fill in each blank with the term that is defined or described.

_____ 1.   A batter that is too thick to be poured but will drop in lumps from a spoon.

_____ 2.   A batter that is liquid enough to be poured.

_____ 3.   A baked product made of a thin batter, leavened only by steam, and characterized by large holes or cavities on the inside.

_____ 4.   The development of elongated holes inside muffin products.

B.   REVIEW OF MIXING METHODS

1.   In the space below, write the procedure for mixing dough by the biscuit method.

2.   In the space below, write the procedure for mixing batters by the muffin method.

3.   In the space below, write the procedure for mixing biscuit doughs by the creaming method.

4. In the space below, write the procedure for mixing muffin batters by the creaming method.

C. USING BAKER'S PERCENTAGES

Use the percentages given to calculate the quantities needed in the following formulas. (You are provided with either the weight of the flour or the total yield by weight.) Fill in the blanks with your answers. Do either the U.S. or Metric calculations or both as indicated by your instructor.

I.

Ingredient	U.S.	%	Metric
Pastry flour	1 lb 11 oz	85%	765 g
Whole wheat flour	5 oz	15%	135 g
Sugar		35%	
Baking powder		6%	
Salt		1.5%	
Pecans		19%	
Eggs 40%		40%	
Milk		60%	
Melted butter		32%	

II.

Milk	_____	200%	_____	
Eggs	_____	125%	_____	
Salt	_____	2%	_____	
Melted butter	_____	13%	_____	
Bread flour	_____	100%	_____	
Yield	2 lb 12 oz	440%	1320 g	

Chapter 9

Doughnuts, Fritters, Pancakes, and Waffles

Some of the techniques you have studied in earlier chapters, including yeast dough production and quick-bread mixing methods, are applied again in this chapter. This chapter discusses a variety of flour-based products that are not baked in the oven.

After studying Chapter 9, you should be able to

1. Prepare doughnuts and other deep-fried desserts and pastries.
2. Prepare pancakes and waffles.
3. Prepare crêpes and crêpe desserts.

A. TERMS

Fill in each blank with the term that is defined or described.

_____   1.   French term for a type of waffle, often made from a thinned-out eclair paste.

_____   2.   A thin, unleavened pancake (French term).

_____   3.   A dessert made from unleavened pancakes, flavored with orange juice and orange liqueur, often flamed.

_____   4.   Pieces of fruit or other food dipped in a batter and deep-fried.

_____   5.   A small piece of eclair paste, fried and served warm, usually with sugar and a sauce.

_____   6.   A doughnut made with eclair paste.

_____   7.   A shiny, transparent icing applied to doughnuts.

_____   8.   Another name (from German) for a jelly-filled doughnut.

B. SHORT ANSWER QUESTIONS

1. Explain why careful control of fermentation times is important when making yeast-raised doughnuts.

   _____

   _____

   _____.

2. What is the proper dough temperature for cake-type doughnuts?

   _____.

3. Why does too low a frying temperature make doughnuts greasy?

   _____.

4. List seven guidelines for the use and care of deep-frying fat.

   (a) _____.

   (b) _____.

   (c) _____.

   (d) _____.

   (e) _____.

   (f) _____.

   (g) _____.

5. After dough for cake doughnuts has been rolled out and cut, what is the next step in the

   procedure before frying the doughnuts? _____.

6.   When doughnuts are coated with confectioners' sugar, should they be warm or cooled? Why?

   _____.

   _____.

7.   What is the usual mixing method for American-style pancakes? _____

   What are the three basic steps in this mixing procedure?

   (a) _____.

   (b) _____.

   (c) _____.

8.   Waffle batter is similar to pancake batter, except that formulas for waffles often call for separating the eggs and whipping the egg whites. What are two other general differences between waffle batter and pancake batter formulas?

   _____

   _____

   _____.

9.   How can you tell when to turn pancakes over to fry the other side?

   _____

   _____.

10.   Why should pancake batter leavened with baking soda be made as close as possible to cooking time?

   _____

   _____.

11. Six suggestions for crêpe desserts are described on page 198 (Crêpes Normande, Banana Crêpes, and so on) and, in addition, 5 full recipes are included on pages 198-202. Invent two additional desserts made with crêpes. Give them names, and describe them in the space below.

C. USING BAKER'S PERCENTAGES

Use the percentages given to calculate the quantities needed in the following formulas. (You are provided with either the weight of the flour or the total yield by weight.) Fill in the blanks with your answers. Do either the U.S. or Metric calculations or both as indicated by your instructor.

I.

Water	_____	55%	_____
Yeast	_____	5%	_____
Shortening	_____	10%	_____
Sugar	_____	14%	_____
Salt	_____	2%	_____
Milk solids	_____	5%	_____
Eggs	_____	14%	_____
Bread flour	_____	100%	_____
Yield	10 lb	205%	5000 g

II.

Pastry flour	1 lb	100%	500 g
Sugar		6%	
Salt		1.5%	
Baking powder		1.5%	
Eggs		50%	
Milk		90%	
Oil		6%	
Vanilla		1%	

Chapter 10

Basic Syrups, Creams, and Sauces

The creams, icings, and sauces introduced in this chapter are fundamental preparations that are essential in a wide variety of pastries, cakes, and desserts. Learn the basic procedures well, because you will need them for the recipes not only in this chapter, but also throughout the rest of the book.

After studying Chapter 10, you should be able to

1. Cook sugar syrups to various stages of hardness.
2. Prepare whipped cream, meringues, custard sauces, and pastry cream variations.
3. Prepare dessert sauces.

A. TERMS

Fill in each blank with the term that is defined or described.

_____ 1. A thick, white foam made of whipped egg whites and sugar.

_____ 2. A foam made by whipping a boiling syrup into whipped egg whites.

_____ 3. A thick custard sauce containing eggs and starch.

_____ 4. A syrup consisting of sucrose and water in various proportions.

_____ 5. A flavored sugar syrup used to flavor and moisten cakes and other desserts.

_____ 6. A rich cream made of sweet chocolate and heavy cream.

_____ 7. The browning of sugars caused by heat.

_____ 8. A foamy sauce or dessert made of egg yolks whipped over heat with wine or liqueur.

_____ 9. A mixture of pastry cream and meringue with flavorings and a gelatin stabilizer.

_____ 10. A sauce made of milk and sugar, thickened with egg yolks and flavored with vanilla.

_____ 11. French term for a sauce made of puréed fruit or other food.

_____ 12. A mixture of pastry cream and whipped cream.

_____ 13. French name for sweetened, vanilla-flavored whipped cream

_____ 14. Egg whites and sugar warmed, usually over hot water, and then whipped to a foam.

B. REVIEW OF SUGAR COOKING

1. A simple syrup consists of _____ pound(s) of _____ dissolved

    in one pint of water.

2. To make a dessert syrup, you add a(n) _____ to a simple syrup.

    Dessert syrups are used to _____

    _____.

3. When melted sugar is heated, it turns brown. This browned sugar is called

    _____.

4. As a syrup is boiled, the concentration of sugar becomes _____,

    and the temperature of the syrup gradually _____.

5. Sometimes an acid, such as _____ or

    _____ is added to a boiling syrup to invert some of the sugar.

    The purpose of doing this is _____

    _____

    _____.

6. What type of sugar should be used for boiled syrups?

    _____.

7. Sugar syrup cooked to a hard crack stage will have a temperature of about

    _____. When this sugar is cooled, its texture will be

    _____.

8. The most accurate way to tell when a syrup has reached the hard ball stage is to

    _____

    _____.

9. When cooking syrups, why should you try to keep sugar from forming crystals on the sides

    of the pan? _____

    _____.

C. REVIEW OF CREAMS, MERINGUES, AND CUSTARDS

1. Why should heavy cream be chilled before whipping? _____

    _____.

2. The first sign that cream is becoming overwhipped is a _____

    _____ appearance. If it continues to be whipped after this stage

    it will _____.

3. To avoid overwhipping cream, stop beating as soon as the cream _____

    _____.

4. To make a stable whipped cream, the best type of sugar to use for sweetening it is

    _____.

5. Whipped cream that is to be mixed with other ingredients should be slightly

    underwhipped, because _____

    _____

    _____.

6. Describe the three basic types of meringues:

(a) Common meringue _____

_____

_____

_____.

(b) Swiss meringue _____

_____

_____

_____.

(c) Italian meringue _____

_____

_____

_____.

7. Egg whites to be whipped should have no trace of yolk in them because

_____.

8. Bowls and beaters for whipping egg whites should be checked carefully, to be

sure they are clean and free of grease, because _____

_____.

9. Properly whipped egg whites are _____ in appearance.

As they are overwhipped they begin to look _____.

10. Cream of tartar is sometimes added to egg whites for whipping because

    _____.

11. Egg whites to be whipped should not be chilled because _____

    _____.

12. The basic ingredients of crème anglaise are _____,

    _____, _____, and _____.

13. Crème anglaise should be cooked until it reaches a temperature of _____.

14. What happens if a crème anglaise is overcooked? _____

    _____.

15. The ingredient that allows pastry cream to be cooked to a higher temperature than crème

    anglaise is _____.

16. The thickening or binding ingredient in crème anglaise is _____.

    The primary thickening ingredient in pastry cream is _____; in addition,

    pastry cream is also thickened with _____.

17. List four sanitation rules to observe when preparing pastry cream. Why is sanitation important when preparing pastry cream?

_____

_____

_____

_____

_____

_____

_____.

18. In its simplest form, ganache is a mixture of _____ and

_____.

19. In the space below, write the procedure for preparing crème anglaise. Use numbered steps.

20. In the space below, write the procedure for preparing vanilla pastry cream. Use numbered steps.

D. USING BAKER'S PERCENTAGES

Use the percentages given to calculate the quantities needed in the following formula. (Note that there is no flour in this formula; the percentages are based on the ingredients indicated.) Fill in the blanks with your answers. Do either the U.S. or Metric calculations or both as indicated by your instructor.

I.

Chocolate at 100%

Sweet chocolate	12 oz	100%	350 g
Butter		50%	
Egg yolks		33%	
Egg whites		75%	
Sugar		16%	

II.

Milk at 100%

Milk	1 lb 4 oz	100%	600 g
Sugar		20%	
Egg yolks		16%	
Cake flour		5%	
Cornstarch		5%	

Chapter 11

Pies

In the first part of this chapter you learn how to make basic pie doughs and to assemble and bake pies. In the second half of the chapter you learn how to make various pie fillings. The review exercises here will help you study this material.

After studying Chapter 11, you should be able to

1. Prepare pie doughs.
2. Roll pie doughs and line pie pans.
3. Fill, assemble, and bake single–crust pies, double–crust pies, and lattice–topped pies.
4. Form and bake pie shells for unbaked pies.
5. Prepare fruit fillings.
6. Prepare soft or custard–type pie fillings.
7. Prepare cream fillings.
8. Prepare chiffon fillings.

A. TERMS

Fill in each blank with the term that is defined or described.

_____ 1. A light, fluffy pie filling containing whipped egg whites and, usually, gelatin.

_____ 2. A liquid that is thickened or set by the coagulation of egg protein.

_____ 3. An unbaked pie containing a pastry-cream-type filling.

_____ 4. A type of canned fruit with very little added water or juice.

_____ 5. A type of canned fruit with no added water.

_____ 6. Referring to canned fruit, the weight of the fruit without the juice.

_____ 7. A type of top crust made of strips of dough laid across each other or interwoven.

_____ 8. A type of starch that will thicken a liquid without being cooked.

B. SHORT-ANSWER QUESTIONS

1. The four basic ingredients of pie dough are _____, _____,

_____, and _____.

2. The two basic types of pie dough are _____ and _____.

3. In the space below, write the procedure for mixing the four ingredients listed in question 1 to make pie dough; use numbered steps. Be sure to explain the difference between the two types of dough named in question 2.

4. If shortening is used to make pie dough, what type of shortening should be used?

   _____.

5. The three basic ingredients of a crumb crust are _____,

   _____, and _____.

6. Two basic types of baked pies are _____ and _____

   _____.

7. Two basic types of unbaked pies are _____ and

   _____.

8.   After a fruit pie filling has been cooked, it should be _____ before filling the

      pie shell and baking.

9.   So that it will not form lumps, a starch must be mixed with _____ or

      _____ before being added to a hot liquid.

10.   Cream pies are thickened with _____.

11.   When rolling out pie dough, it is best to use as little flour as possible for dusting, because

      _____

      _____.

12.   Fruit pies are baked at a _____ (high *or* low) temperature so that

      _____.

      _____.

13.   The best type of pie dough to use for pumpkin pies is _____.

14.   The cooking method most often used to make pie fillings from canned fruit is the

      _____.

15.   The cooking method most often used to make pie fillings from fresh, raw fruit is the

      _____.

16. Raw pineapple should not be mixed with gelatin because _____

_____.

C. PIE FILLING PROCEDURE REVIEW

1. In the space below, explain how to make fruit pie fillings using the cooked fruit method. Write the procedure in the form of numbered steps.

2. In the space below, explain how to make fruit pie fillings using the cooked juice method. Write the procedure in the form of numbered steps.

3. In the space below, write a general procedure for preparing chiffon pie fillings.

4. In the space below, write the procedure for preparing lemon pie filling. Use numbered steps.

D. USING BAKER'S PERCENTAGES

Use the percentages given to calculate the quantities needed in the following formulas. (You are provided with either the weight of the flour or the total yield by weight.) Fill in the blanks with your answers. Do either the U.S. or Metric calculations or both as indicated by your instructor.

I.

Pastry flour	_____	100%	_____
Shortening	_____	67%	_____
Water	_____	28%	_____
Salt	_____	1.5%	_____
Sugar	_____	4%	_____
Yield	5 lb	200%	2500 g

II.

Pastry flour	2 lb	100%	900 g
Sugar	_____	17%	_____
Butter	_____	50%	_____
Egg yolks	_____	8%	_____
Water, cold	_____	25%	_____
Salt	_____	1%	_____

Chapter 12

Pastry Basics

Pastries, cakes, and breads are the fundamental products of the bakeshop. This chapter presents the most important types of pastry doughs, with the exception of pie doughs, which are covered in Chapter 11. You will learn to mix these doughs and to make various simple baked goods with them. In the next chapter, you will learn to use these doughs to make more elaborate pastries.

After studying Chapter 12, you should be able to

1. Prepare pâte brisée and short pastries.
2. Prepare puff pastry dough, blitz puff pastry dough, and reversed puff pastry doughs, and prepare simple pastries from these doughs.
3. Prepare pâte à choux (éclair paste), and prepare simple pastries from it.
4. Prepare strudel dough, handle commercial phyllo (strudel) dough, and prepare pastries using either homemade or commercial dough.
5. Bake meringue and meringue-type sponges, and assemble simple desserts with these meringues.

A. TERMS

Fill in each blank with the term that is defined or described.

_____   1.   A type of rich pastry dough, similar to cookie dough, made with butter, sugar, and eggs, and used for tart shells.

_____   2.   French name for éclair paste.

_____   3.   A crisp disk of baked meringue containing nuts.

_____   4.   A dessert made of crisp baked meringues and ice cream.

_____   5.   Tiny cream puffs, often filled with ice cream and served with chocolate syrup.

_____   6.   A dessert made of layers of puff pastry alternating with layers of pastry cream or other cream or filling.

_____   7.   A type of dough that is mixed like pie dough but rolled and folded like puff paste.

_____   8.   A tart of caramelized apples, baked with the pastry on top, then turned upside down for display and service.

_____   9.   A paper-thin dough or pastry used to make strudels and various Middle Eastern and Greek desserts.

_____   10.   French name for a type of rich pastry dough, similar to a pie dough made with egg.

_____   11.   A type of dough that is stretched until it is paper-thin.

B. TRUE OR FALSE

T   F   1.   Bread flour is the preferred flour for éclair paste.

T   F   2.   Danish dough and puff pastry dough are both rolled-in doughs, but Danish dough is leavened with yeast, while puff pastry dough is not.

T   F   3.   Puff pastry products are baked at low temperatures to prevent burning or scorching.

T   F   4.   Touching the edges of cut puff pastry dough units before baking may cause the layers to stick together at the edges and rise unevenly when baked.

T   F   5.   Butter to be rolled into puff paste must be well chilled and hard so that it will not ooze out of the dough.

T   F   6.   Eclair paste should be deposited on well greased pans for baking.

T   F   7.   When éclair paste is mixed the eggs should be added all at once.

T   F   8.   Puff pastry, éclair paste, and popover batter all depend on the same leavening agent.

T   F   9.   Strudel dough is mixed well to develop strong gluten.

T   F   10.   Strudel dough should be chilled well before stretching.

T   F   11.   Pâte sablée is a type of puff pastry dough that can be made more quickly than classic puff pastry.

T   F   12.   Short dough can be considered a type of cookie dough.

T   F   13.   The quantity of rolled-in fat used for puff pastry may vary from 50 to 100% of the weight of the flour.

T   F   14   Unlike Danish dough, which is given three-folds or simple turns, puff pastry dough is always given four-folds.

C. PROCEDURE REVIEW

1. In the space below, write the basic procedure for making éclair paste. Use numbered steps.

2. In the space below, write the basic procedure for making pâte brisée. Use numbered steps.

3. In the space below, write a basic procedure for making puff pastry, beginning with the mixed dough and the block of butter. You may use any of the procedures in the text or the one preferred by your instructor. Use numbered steps.

D. USING BAKER'S PERCENTAGES

Use the percentages given to calculate the quantities needed in the following formulas. (You are provided with either the weight of the flour or the total yield by weight.) Fill in the blanks with your answers. Do either the U.S. or Metric calculations or both as indicated by your instructor.

I.

Ingredient	U.S.	Percent	Metric
Pastry flour	7 lb	100%	3200 g
Sugar		17%	
Butter		50%	
Egg yolks		8%	
Water		25%	
Salt		1%	

II.

Ingredient	U.S.	Percent	Metric
Butter		67%	
Sugar		25%	
Salt		0.5%	
Eggs		20%	
Pastry flour		100%	
Yield:	5 lb	212%	2500 g

Chapter 13

Tarts and
Special Pastries

This is the second of two chapters on pastry. Chapter 12 presents the most important pastry doughs and other preparations used in pastries. This chapter introduces you to a variety of tarts and then gives examples of a variety of other sophisticated pastries. These give you further practice using the doughs from Chapter 12 and also give you the opportunity to develop your decorative skills.

After studying Chapter 13, you should be able to

1. Prepare bake and unbaked tarts and tartlets.
2. Prepare a variety of special pastries based on puff pastry, choux pastry, and meringue-type pastry.

A. TERMS

Fill in each blank with the term that is defined or described.

_____ 1. A tart made of raspberry jam and a short dough containing nuts and spices.

_____ 2. A tart of caramelized apples, baked with the pastry on top and then turned upside down for display and service.

_____ 3. A dessert made of a ring of cream puffs set on a short dough base and filled with crème chiboust or crème diplomat.

_____ 4. A pastry made of two layers of puff paste enclosing an almond filling.

_____ 5. A flat, baked item consisting of a pastry and a sweet or savory topping or filling; similar to a pie but usually thinner.

_____ 6. A dessert of the type described in number 5, with a filling of custard and prunes.

_____ 7. A southern Italian turnover pastry with a sweet cheese filling.

_____ 8. Any of a variety of small fancy cakes and other pastries, usually in single-portion sizes.

B. SHORT-ANSWER QUESTIONS

1. Tart shells baked without a filling are docked before baking because

   _____.

2. Why is it important to select a dough with a good flavor when making tarts?

   _____

   _____.

3. The simplest kind of baked fruit tart consists of _____

   _____.

4. Sometimes cake crumbs are spread on the bottom of a tart shell before the fruit is added and the tart is baked. What is the purpose of using crumbs?

   _____

   _____.

5. In the space below, write the procedure for making baked tart shells. Use numbered steps.

6. If a fruit is too hard to be cooked completely when baked in a tart, what can you do to ensure that it will become tender? _____

_____

_____.

7. In the space below, write a procedure for making a simple, unbaked, fresh raspberry tart. Use numbered steps.

Chapter 14

Cake Mixing and Baking

Because cakes are some of the most delicate products a baker makes, it is important to mix and bake them with a great deal of precision and care. This chapter will help you study the mixing and baking methods for many types of cakes.

After studying Chapter 14, you should be able to

1. Perform basic cake mixing methods.
2. Produce high-fat or shortened cakes, including high-ratio cakes and cakes mixed by creaming.
3. Produce foam-type cakes, including sponge, angel food, and chiffon cakes.
4. Scale and bake cakes correctly.
5. Correct cake failures or defects.

A. TERMS

Fill in each blank with the term that is defined or described.

_____ 1. A type of cake based on an egg-white foam and containing no fat.

_____ 2. A cake made of equal parts butter, sugar, flour, and eggs.

_____ 3. A general term for cakes made with whole-egg foams or egg-yolk foams.

_____ 4. A cake made of a whole-egg-and-sugar foam, flour, and sometimes melted butter, but no other liquid.

_____ 5. A type of cake made with an egg-white foam and oil.

_____ 6. A uniform mixture of two unmixable substances.

_____ 7. A cake mixing method that begins with the blending of fat and sugar.

_____ 8. A cake mixing method that requires the use of emulsified shortening.

_____ 9. A cake made by adding one thin layer of batter at a time to a pan and browning under a broiler or salamander.

_____ 10. A thin cake layer decorated with a baked-in design made with stencil paste.

B. SHORT-ANSWER QUESTIONS

1. If shortening is used to make old-fashioned pound cake, mixed by the creaming method, the correct shortening to use is _____.

2. Ingredients for a high-fat or shortened cake should be at _____ temperature for mixing.

3. The term "high-ratio," when applied to cakes, means that the weight of the _____ in the formula is greater than the weight of the _____.

4. List five factors that can cause curdling or separation of ingredients when mixing high-fat cakes.

   (a) _____

   _____.

   (b) _____

   _____.

   (c) _____

   _____.

   (d) _____

   _____.

   (e) _____

   _____.

5. Overmixing is likely to make a cake's texture _____ because of gluten development.

6. Most cakes are made with _____ (strong *or* weak) flour.

7. Proper mixing speed for two-stage cakes is _____.

8. The two-stage method gets its name because the _____ ingredients are added in two stages.

9. The primary leavening agent for genoise is _____.

10. Describe the texture of egg whites that have been properly whipped for angel food cake,

    _____

    _____

    _____.

11. For the purpose of balancing cake formulas, ingredients can be classified according to four functions: _____, _____,

    _____, and _____.

12. In the spaces following each of the ingredients below, write the names of the functions which that ingredient fills. (Use the four functions that you listed in question 11. Note that an ingredient may fill more than one function.)

Flour: _____

Sugar: _____

Eggs: _____

Water: _____

Liquid milk: _____

Nonfat milk solids: _____

Butter: _____

Shortening: _____

Baking powder: _____

Cocoa powder: _____

13. List three ways to determine when a high-fat cake is done baking.

(a) _____

_____.

(b) _____

_____.

(c) _____

_____.

C. REVIEW OF CAKE MIXING METHODS

1. In the space below, write a procedure for mixing cakes by the creaming method. Use numbered steps.

2. In the space below, write a procedure for mixing cakes by the two-stage method. Use numbered steps.

3. In the space below, write a procedure for mixing genoise cakes. Use numbered steps.

4. In the space below, write a procedure for mixing angel food cakes. Use numbered steps.

5. In the space below, write a procedure for mixing chiffon cakes. Use numbered steps.

D. USING BAKER'S PERCENTAGES

Use the percentages given to calculate the quantities needed in the following formulas. (You are provided with either the weight of the flour or the total yield by weight.) Fill in the blanks with your answers. Do either the U.S. or Metric calculations or both as indicated by your instructor.

I.

Sugar	_____	95%	_____
Shortening	_____	20%	_____
Butter	_____	10%	_____
Salt	_____	1%	_____
Cinnamon	_____	0.5%	_____
Eggs	_____	20%	_____
Skim milk	_____	38%	_____
Cake flour	_____	100%	_____
Baking powder	_____	2.5%	_____
Baking soda	_____	2.5%	_____
Chopped apples	_____	100%	_____
Yield	_____5 lb_____	389%	_____2334 g_____

II.

Sugar	_____	125%	_____
Whole eggs	_____	75%	_____
Egg yolks	_____	25%	_____
Salt	_____	1.5%	_____
Cake flour	2 lb 8 oz	100%	1200 g
Baking powder	_____	3%	_____
Skim milk	_____	50%	_____
Butter	_____	25%	_____
Vanilla	_____	3%	_____

Chapter 15

Assembling and Decorating Cakes

This chapter forms a unit with Chapters 14 and 16. Together they explain the production, assembly, and decoration of a great variety of cakes. This chapter begins with a discussion of icings. It then proceeds to the basic procedures for assembling and icing the basic baked products to make attractive desserts. It introduces some of the more artistic aspects of cake production. Careful practice and repetition, with an instructor's guidance, are essential if you are to develop skill.

After studying Chapter 15, you should be able to

1. Prepare icings.
2. Assemble and ice simple layer cakes, sheet cakes, and cupcakes.
3. Make and use a paper decorating cone.
4. Use a pastry bag to make simple icing decorations.

A. TERMS

Fill in each blank with the term that is defined or described.

_____ 1. A form of icing made of confectioners' sugar and egg whites; used for decorating.

_____ 2. An icing made of butter and/or shortening blended with confectioners' sugar or sugar syrup, and sometimes other ingredients.

_____ 3. A mixture of confectioners' sugar and water, sometimes with other ingredients, used as an icing.

_____ 4. An icing made of meringue and gelatin.

_____ 5. A sugar syrup that is crystallized to a smooth, creamy white mass; used as an icing.

_____ 6. A sponge cake or other yellow cake filled with pastry cream and topped with chocolate fondant.

_____ 7. A pedestal with a flat, rotating top, used for holding cakes while they are being iced.

_____ 8. A plastic triangle with toothed or serrated edges, used for texturing icings.

_____ 9. A variety of small fancy cakes and other pastries, usually in single-portion sizes.

_____ 10. To partly mix two colors of icing to make a decorative pattern.

_____ 11. A transparent, sweet jelly used for decorating cakes.

B. REVIEW OF ICINGS

1. What are the three main functions of icings?

   (a) _____.

   (b) _____.

   (c) _____.

2. For use, fondant should be heated to a temperature of _____.

   It should not be heated more than this because _____

   _____.

3. The two basic ingredients of simple buttercream are _____

   and _____.

4. Describe how to make decorator's buttercream. What is it used for?

   _____

   _____

   _____

   _____.

5. In the space that follows, describe how to make French buttercream.

6. What is the difference between plain boiled icing and Italian meringue?

    _____

    _____

    _____.

7. What is the difference between boiled icing and marshmallow icing?

    _____

    _____.

8. Describe how to make and store royal icing.

    _____

    _____

    _____

    _____

    _____.

C. REVIEW OF CAKE ASSEMBLY

1. In the space below, describe how to assemble and ice a simple American-style layer cake. Use numbered steps.

2. In the space below, describe how to turn out, ice, and decorate a simple sheet cake with marked portions. Use numbered steps.

3. Briefly describe each of the following decorating techniques:

(a)   stenciling

(b)   marbling

(c)   palette knife patterns

(d)   masking the sides of the cake

(e)   piping jelly transfers

D. USING BAKER'S PERCENTAGES

Use the percentages given to calculate the quantities needed in the following formula. (Note that there is no flour in this formula; the percentages are based on the ingredients indicated.) Fill in the blanks with your answers. Do either the U.S. or Metric calculations or both as indicated by your instructor.

Sugar at 100%

	U.S.		Metric
Sugar	1 lb 4 oz	100%	600 g
Water		25%	
Egg yolks		37.5%	
Butter		125%	
Vanilla		1.5%	

105

Chapter 16

Specialty Cakes, Gâteaux, and Torten

This is the third of three chapters on cake baking, assembly, and decoration. In this chapter you are introduced to more advanced techniques that will enable you to assemble elegant gâteaux and other specialty cakes. The photographs accompanying the many examples will help you visualize these creations as you duplicate them.

After studying Chapter 16, you should be able to

1. Select from a variety of components to plan cakes that have well-balanced flavors and textures.
2. Line Charlotte rings or cake rings for specialty cakes.
3. Coat a cake with marzipan.
4. Assemble a variety of European-style cakes, Swiss rolls, small cakes, and petits fours.

A. TERMS

Fill in each blank with the term that is defined or described.

_____ 1. German word for various types of cakes, usually layer cakes.

_____ 2. A rich chocolate cake coated with apricot jam and chocolate fondant icing.

_____ 3. A small, bite-size, iced cake.

_____ 4. A layer cake iced and filled with coffee-flavored buttercream.

_____ 5. A thin sheet of sponge cake spread with a filling and rolled up.

_____ 6. French word for cake.

_____ 7. A chocolate sponge cake flavored with kirsch and filled with cherries and whipped cream.

_____ 8. A layer cake consisting of a top and bottom layer of baked meringue and a middle layer of sponge cake flavored with kirsch syrup.

_____ 9. A sponge layer cake iced with a macaroon mixture and browned in the oven.

_____ 10. A cake made of seven thin layers filled with chocolate buttercream and topped with caramelized sugar.

_____ 11. A cake roll decorated to look like a log.

_____ 12. A type of small (single-portion size), spherical sponge cake filled with cream and iced with fondant.

_____ 13. A layer cake made of thin sponge layers, coffee-flavored buttercream, and chocolate ganache.

_____ 14. A metal ring used as a mold for charlottes and cakes.

B. REVIEW OF CAKE ASSEMBLY

1. In the space below, describe how to assemble a basic layered sponge cake. Use numbered steps.

2. In the space below, describe how to line a ring mold with a sponge strip. Use numbered steps.

3. In the space below, use numbered steps to describe in detail how to assemble the following elements into a European-style layer cake.

    Base: chocolate meringue disk
    Cake: chocolate genoise, split into 2 layers
    Syrup: vanilla-flavored
    Filling: chocolate mousse
    Icing: chocolate buttercream

Chapter 17

Cookies

Learning to make cookies easily and efficiently is mainly a matter of developing manual skills. The portion of the chapter devoted to theory and basic principles is relatively short, but it includes material that you should study well. This chapter will help you review that material.

After studying Chapter 17, you should be able to

1. Understand the causes of crispness, chewiness, and spread in cookies.
2. Prepare cookie doughs by the three basic methods.
3. Prepare eight basic types of cookies: dropped, bagged, rolled, molded, icebox, bar, sheet, and stencil.
4. Bake and cool cookies properly.

A. TERMS

Fill in each blank with the term that is defined or described.

_____	1.	A cookie made of coconut mixed with meringue.
_____	2.	An uniced or unfilled petit four, such as a small butter cookie.
_____	3.	Cookies sliced from refrigerated, cylinder-shaped pieces of dough.
_____	4.	Cookies pressed from a pastry bag.
_____	5.	A rich Scottish cookie made of butter, flour, and sugar; some variations also contain egg.
_____	6.	Cookies made with a cookie cutter.
_____	7.	Cookies made from equal pieces of dough cut from a cylinder and then shaped.
_____	8.	Cookies made by spreading dough or batter in sheet pans, baking, and then cutting out squares or rectangles.
_____	9.	Finger-shaped soft cookies made from a sponge batter.
_____	10.	Readily absorbing moisture.
_____	11.	Cookies made from cylinders of dough placed on sheet pans, baked, then cut crosswise into pieces.
_____	12.	Cookies made from lumps of dough dropped onto baking pans.
_____	13.	A pattern cut from plastic or cardboard, used for depositing batter for thin cookies made in decorative shapes.
_____	14.	Crisp, Italian-style cookies made by the bar method and baked twice.

B. SHORT-ANSWER QUESTIONS

1. All the cookies in each batch should be made uniform in shape and size because

    _____

    _____.

2. In order to prevent rich cookies from burning too easily on the bottom when baked, the

    baker can _____

    _____.

3. What may happen to cookies that are cooled too rapidly?

    _____.

4. Cookie doneness is indicated primarily by _____.

5. Five factors that contribute to crispness in cookies are:

    (a) _____.

    (b) _____.

    (c) _____.

    (d) _____.

    (e) _____.

6. Six factors that contribute to softness in cookies are:

(a) _____.

(b) _____.

(c) _____.

(d) _____.

(e) _____.

(f) _____.

7. For each of the following, indicate whether it increases or decreases a cookie's tendency to spread when baked:

(a) High sugar content _____

(b) Using confectioners' sugar instead of granulated _____

(c) Low baking temperature _____

(d) Not greasing the baking sheet _____

(e) Excessive creaming _____

(f) High liquid content in batter _____

(g) Use of strong flour _____

(h) High baking powder content _____

8. A cookie mixing method that begins with whipping eggs and sugar to a foam is a

_____ method.

9. When cookies are rolled out with a rolling pin, no more flour than necessary should be used for dusting, because _____

    _____.

10. How does the egg content of a cookie mix affect the chewiness of the cookie?

    _____

    _____.

C. REVIEW OF COOKIE MIXING METHODS

1. Using numbered steps, describe the creaming method for mixing cookies.

2. Using numbered steps, describe the one-stage method for mixing cookies.

D. USING BAKER'S PERCENTAGES

Use the percentages given to calculate the quantities needed in the following formulas. (You are provided with either the weight of the flour or the total yield by weight.) Fill in the blanks with your answers. Do either the U.S. or Metric calculations or both as indicated by your instructor.

I.

Butter	_____	67%	_____
Brown sugar	_____	133%	_____
Salt	_____	1.5%	_____
Eggs	_____	33%	_____
Vanilla	_____	3%	_____
Milk	_____	8%	_____
Pastry flour	_____	100%	_____
Baking powder	_____	4%	_____
Baking soda	_____	2%	_____
Rolled oats	_____	83%	_____
Raisins	_____	67%	_____
Yield	11 lb	501%	5110 g

117

II.

Butter		90%	
Granulated sugar		50%	
Confectioners' sugar		40%	
Egg whites		65%	
Vanilla		1.5%	
Cake flour	1 lb 8 oz	75%	750 g
Bread flour	8 oz	25%	250 g

Chapter 18

Custards, Puddings, Mousses, and Soufflés

This chapter presents a wide variety of techniques and products. Many of these preparations are based on some of the techniques you have already learned. In particular, you should review the information on various custards and creams in Chapter 10. These are fundamental techniques that you should know well.

After studying Chapter 18, you should be able to

1. Prepare starch–thickened or boiled puddings.
2. Prepare baked custards and baked puddings.
3. Prepare steamed puddings.
4. Prepare Bavarian creams and mousses.
5. Use Bavarian creams to prepare charlottes.
6. Prepare hot dessert soufflés.

A. TERMS

Fill in each blank with the term that is defined or described.

_____ 1. A soft or creamy dessert that is made light by the addition of whipped cream, egg whites, or both.

_____ 2. A baked dish containing whipped egg whites, which cause the dish to rise during baking.

_____ 3. A light, cold dessert made of gelatin, whipped cream, and crème anglaise or fruit.

_____ 4. A liquid that is thickened or set by the coagulation of egg protein.

_____ 5. An English boiled pudding made of milk, sugar, and cornstarch.

_____ 6. A custard baked in a mold lined with caramel, then unmolded.

_____ 7. A baked custard with a brittle top made of caramelized sugar.

_____ 8. A steamed pudding made of dried and candied fruits, spices, beef suet, and crumbs.

_____ 9. A cold dessert made of Bavarian cream or other cream in a special mold, usually lined with ladyfingers or other sponge product.

_____ 10. A rich baked custard served in a small cup.

_____ 11. A rich rice pudding containing whipped cream, candied fruits, and gelatin.

_____ 12. An Italian pudding made of cream, sugar, gelatin, and flavorings.

B. TRUE OR FALSE

T	F	1.	Crème anglaise and baked custard are made of basically the same ingredients, but the cooking methods are different.
T	F	2.	When scalded milk is added to egg yolks it should be added all at once.
T	F	3.	Blanc mange should not be heated to more than 185° F (85° C) during cooking.
T	F	4.	Cream puddings, such as vanilla pudding, are prepared using the same procedure as for making pastry cream.
T	F	5.	Butterscotch pudding is made by making vanilla pudding with extra butter and adding scotch flavoring.
T	F	6.	Crème brûlée is usually richer than crème caramel because crème brûlée is made with heavy cream instead of milk.
T	F	7.	Pumpkin pie filling and baked cheesecake are custards.
T	F	8.	Bavarian creams are similar to mousses, but they are firmer because of their gelatin content.
T	F	9.	If both whipped cream and whipped egg whites must be added to a chocolate mousse, the whipped cream is always added first.
T	F	10.	An appropriate temperature for baking a soufflé is 375° F (190° C).

C. PROCEDURE REVIEW

1. In the space below, write the procedure for making vanilla Bavarian cream. Use numbered steps.

2. In the space below, write the procedure for making a simple baked custard. Use numbered steps.

3. In the space below, name the three basic components of a baked dessert soufflé. Explain each component, giving examples where appropriate.

4. In the space below, write the procedure for making vanilla-flavored panna cotta. Use numbered steps.

Chapter 19

Frozen Desserts

The frozen desserts, including ice creams, that are presented in this chapter use many of the same techniques as those in the previous chapters. For example, crème anglaise is the basis for ice cream and many frozen mousses, just as it is for the Bavarian creams in Chapter 18. And like Bavarians and mousses, still-frozen desserts depend on whipped cream or egg foams for their light texture. You might consider this chapter a continuation of Chapter 18.

After studying Chapter 19, you should be able to

1. Judge the quality of commercial ice creams.
2. Prepare ice creams and sorbets.
3. Prepare ice cream and sorbet desserts using commercial or homemade ice creams and sorbets.
4. Prepare still-frozen desserts, including bombes, frozen mousses, and frozen soufflés.

A. TERMS

Fill in each blank with the term that is defined or described.

_____ 1. A type of frozen dessert made in a dome-shaped mold and usually consisting of two or more layers.

_____ 2. The increase in volume of ice cream or frozen desserts due to the incorporation of air while freezing.

_____ 3. A frozen dessert usually made of water, sugar, fruit juice or purée, and sometimes egg whites, milk, or cream.

_____ 4. A frozen dessert similar to that described in number 3, but with a coarse, crystalline texture.

_____ 5. A dessert consisting of a peach half and raspberry sauce on top of vanilla ice cream.

_____ 6. Ice cream made without eggs.

_____ 7. A frozen dessert similar to ice cream but made with milk and no cream.

_____ 8. A dessert consisting of one or two scoops of ice cream or sherbet in a dish or glass topped with any of a number of syrups, fruits, or toppings.

_____ 9. A dessert consisting of ice cream on a sponge cake base, covered with meringue and browned in the oven.

_____ 10. A dessert consisting of a pear half, chocolate sauce, and toasted almonds over vanilla ice cream.

_____ 11. A dessert consisting of alternating layers of ice cream and fruit or syrup in a tall, narrow glass.

_____ 12. A still-frozen dessert made in a tall, narrow mold.

126

B. SHORT ANSWER QUESTIONS

1. What is overrun? How does it affect the quality of ice cream?

   _____

   _____

   _____

2. What are five factors that affect overrun?

   _____

   _____

   _____

   _____

   _____

   _____.

3. For storage, ice cream should be kept at a temperature of _____ or lower.

   For serving, it should be brought to a temperature of _____.

4. Why are careful sanitation procedures important when you are making ice cream?

   _____

   _____

   _____.

5. In the space below, write the procedure for making vanilla ice cream using egg yolks. Use numbered steps.

6. In the space below, write the procedure for making a frozen mousse with a meringue base. Use numbered steps.

7. In the space below, write the procedure for making a frozen mousse with a custard base. Use numbered steps.

Chapter 20

Fruit Desserts

Chapter 20 begins with a discussion of the characteristics, quality factors, and basic preparation procedures of fresh fruits. The list includes common fruits as well as exotic specialty fruits. The remainder of the chapter is devoted to a selection of fruit desserts and various garnishes and condiments made of fruit.

After studying Chapter 20, you should be able to

1. Select good-quality fresh fruits and prepare them for use in desserts.
2. Prepare various fruit desserts, including poached fruits and fruit compotes.

A. TERMS

Fill in each blank with the term that is defined or described.

_____   1.   A dish consisting of sweetened, sliced apples
                               baked with a streusel or crumb topping.

_____   2.   Fresh or dried fruit poached in a syrup.

_____   3.   A dessert made of fruit baked with a pastry
                               crust on top.

_____   4.   A dessert made by layering fruit and cake
                               crumbs in a pan and then baking.

_____   5.   A hot dessert consisting of apples baked in a
                               mold lined with buttered slices of bread.

B. SHORT ANSWER QUESTIONS

1.   List 4 fruits that will darken when cut and exposed to air. _____,

      _____, _____, _____.

      How can you prevent this browning? _____

      _____.

2.   Why is it not advisable to refrigerate bananas? _____.

3.   Describe the best way to store, handle, and clean fresh raspberries

      _____.

4,   What type of fruit dessert resembles a pie without a bottom crust? _____.

5.   Describe in general terms how to prepare a peach compote (poached peaches) for use as a
      dessert.

6. Peach crisp consists of sweetened sliced peaches baked with a topping of

_____.

7. What piece of equipment is used to finish a fruit gratin before serving?

_____.

8. The thickening or binding agent used for jams and marmalades is _____.

Chapter 21

Dessert Presentation

Unlike most of the other chapters you have studied, this chapter contains no mixing method or baking procedures. Rather it is devoted primarily to suggestions for various platings. The chapter begins with some general guidelines to help you design attractive presentations of desserts. Study the guidelines and the individual examples, and then let your imagination work.

After studying Chapter 21, you should be able to

Plate and serve attractive presentations of desserts with appropriate sauces and garnishes.

A. TERMS

Fill in each blank with the term that is defined or described.

_____ 1. French term for a spoonful of ice cream or other food shaped into an oval.

_____ 2. Decorative edible item used to complement or enhance the eye appeal of another food item.

_____ 3. To partly mix two colors of sauce to make a decorative pattern.

_____ 4. The presentation or plating of a single portion of a dessert item, with or without sauce or garnish.

_____ 5. A dessert plating that includes two or more desserts (main items) on a plate, plus optional sauces and garnish.

B. DESSERT PRESENTATIONS

Following the principles outlined in Chapter 19 of the textbook, draw diagrams of four dessert presentations. In the blanks provided, indicate the main items, garnishes, and sauces you are using. Make your own selections (from recipes in the textbook or from class handouts or other sources) or whatever items are assigned by your instructor. For the first two presentations draw the diagrams in the large circles, which represent round plates. For the second two presentations no plate outlines are provided. Draw plates of any shape desired or assigned (round, oval, square, and so on).

The following simple example shows you the method. This is a diagram of the dessert described on page 554.

Main item(s) ___strawberry cream cake___

_____

_____

Garnish(es) _____

_____

_____

Sauce(s) ___strawberry, marbled_____

_____

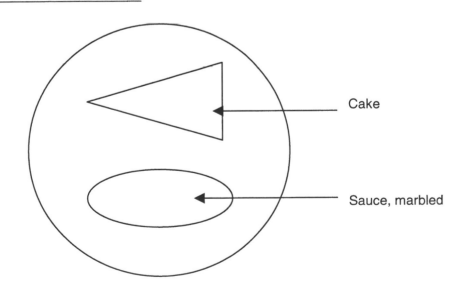

Main item(s) _____

_____

_____

Garnish(es) _____

_____

_____

Sauce(s) _____

_____

Main item(s) _____

_____

_____

Garnish(es) _____

_____

_____

Sauce(s) _____

_____

Main item(s) _____

_____

_____

Garnish(es) _____

_____

_____

Sauce(s) _____

_____

Main item(s) _____

_____

_____

Garnish(es) _____

_____

_____

Sauce(s) _____

_____

Chapter 22

Chocolate

The last three chapters of the textbook introduce you to some advanced decorative techniques, many of which are very difficult and require demonstration and guidance from your instructor, followed by a great deal of practice. The first of these three chapters explains how to work with chocolate in order to make decorative items and confections.

After studying Chapter 22, you should be able to

1. Temper chocolate couverture.
2. Use tempered chocolate for dipping and molding.
3. Produce a variety of chocolate decorations.
4. Make chocolate truffles.

A. TERMS

Fill in each blank with the term that is defined or described.

_____ 1. A whitish coating on chocolate, caused by separated cocoa butter.

_____ 2. Natural, sweet chocolate containing no added fats other than natural cocoa butter; used for dipping, molding, coating, and similar purposes.

_____ 3. A thick paste made of chocolate and glucose, which can be molded by hand into various shapes.

_____ 4. The process of melting and cooling chocolate in order to prepare it for molding or dipping.

_____ 5. The process, in the manufacturing of chocolate, of grinding together cocoa, cocoa butter, and sugar in order to create a fine, smooth texture.

_____ 6. A method for carrying out the process described in number 4 by spreading the melted chocolate back and forth on a marble slab.

_____ 7. The fat component of natural chocolate.

_____ 8. Unsweetened chocolate consisting of cocoa solids plus the substance described in number 7.

B. SHORT ANSWER QUESTIONS

1. Melted chocolate that is to be used for dipping can be thinned out by adding

_____.

2. The two basic components of unsweetened chocolate are _____ and

_____.

3. The three basic components of sweet chocolate are _____,

   _____, and _____.

4. The four basic components of milk chocolate are _____,

   _____, _____, and _____.

5. To temper chocolate, first melt it and bring it to a temperature of _____

   _____.

6. After the chocolate is melted, the next stage of tempering is to _____

   _____.

7. Finally, to prepare the tempered chocolate for dipping or molding, it should be

   _____

   _____.

8. If a whitish coating appears on the cooled chocolate, it probably means that, during

   the step described in number 7, the chocolate was _____

   _____.

9. If chocolate that has been tempered takes too long to harden, it probably means that

   _____

   _____.

10. When dipping chocolates, a good temperature for the work area is

_____.

11. Briefly describe how to dip candies using a dipping fork in order to coat them with chocolate.

_____

_____

_____.

12. Piping chocolate is made of tempered chocolate mixed with _____

until it forms the proper consistency.

13. Describe how to make modeling chocolate. _____

_____

_____

_____.

14. How should chocolate molds be prepared to ensure that they are clean and free of

scratches? _____

_____

_____.

15. Why can chocolate usually be removed from molds easily (providing the molds have

been prepared well and are in good condition)? _____

_____

_____.

16. If you spilled a few drops of water into chocolate while it is being melted, it would

_____.

17. Very simple chocolate truffles can be made out of only two ingredients,

_____ and _____.

Chapter 23

Decorative Work: Marzipan, Nougatine, and Pastillage

Your study of decorative work continues in this chapter with marzipan, nougatine, and pastillage. The first two are not only used for purely decorative work; they can also be used to make edible confections, garnish, and components for many kinds of desserts. Pastillage, on the other hand, even though it is made out of edible ingredients, is used only for decorations and display pieces. It is not intended to be eaten.

After studying Chapter 23, you should be able to

1. Make and handle marzipan, and mold decorative items from it.
2. Make pastillage and use it to create decorative items.
3. Make nougatine and shape it into simple decorative items.

A. TERMS

Fill in each blank with the term that is defined or described.

_____ 1. A sugar paste made of sugar, starch, and gelatin, which is used for decorative work, and which becomes hard and brittle when dry.

_____ 2. A mixture of caramelized sugar and almonds or other nuts; used in decorative work and as a confection and flavoring.

_____ 3. The material described in number 1, but made with vegetable gums instead of gelatin.

_____ 4. A paste or confection made of ground almonds and sugar, often used for decorative work.

B. MARZIPAN REVIEW

1. In the space below, list the ingredients for making marzipan. Then describe the procedure for making marzipan, using numbered steps.

2. When working with pastry doughs, you use flour to dust the work surface. When working

   with marzipan, you use _____ to dust the work surface.

3. Mixing bowls for marzipan should be made of _____.

   The reason for this is _____

   _____.

4. How should marzipan be stored? _____

   _____.

C. REVIEW OF PASTILLAGE AND NOUGATINE

1. In the space below, list the ingredients for making pastillage. Then describe the procedure for making pastillage, using numbered steps.

2. Mixing bowls for making pastillage should be made of _____.

    The reason for this is _____

    _____.

3. When working with pastillage, the work surface should be dusted with

    _____.

4. When working with pastillage, unused portions should be stored by _____

    _____

    _____.

5. Describe a simple method for making a pastillage bowl. _____

    _____

    _____

    _____.

6. How should molded pastillage pieces be dried? _____

    _____.

7. If a pastillage showpiece is made of more than one piece, the parts are fastened together by

    _____.

8. Nougatine pieces are fastened together by _____

_____.

9. The two main ingredients in nougatine are _____

and _____.

10. The best work surface for rolling and cutting nougatine is a(n) _____.

The next best choice is a(n) _____that has been

_____ so that the nougatine won't stick.

11. The basic tool for cutting nougatine is _____.

12. Nougatine can be molded like pastillage, but if it becomes too hard to mold it can be

softened by _____

_____.

Chapter 24

Decorative Work: Sugar Techniques

Pastry chefs often consider decorative sugar work to be one of the pinnacles of their art. In this chapter you are introduced to the fine art of making beautiful display pieces with pulled and blown sugar. In addition, you learn to use boiled sugar to make a number of simple, practical items that aren't as challenging as pulled sugar and that can be used every day to create interesting decorations and garnishes.

After studying Chapter 24, you should be able to

1. Boil sugar syrups correctly got decorative sugar works.
2. Make spun sugar, sugar cages, and poured sugar.
3. Pull sugar and use it to make simple pulled and blown sugar decorative items.

A. TERMS

Fill in each blank with the term that is defined or described.

_____ 1. Sugar that is boiled to the hard-crack stage, allowed to harden slightly, then pulled or stretched until it develops a pearly sheen.

_____ 2. The material described in number 1, which is then made into hollow shapes by being blown up like a balloon.

_____ 3. Boiled sugar made into fine, hairlike threads.

_____ 4. Sugar that is boiled to the hard-crack stage and then poured into molds to harden.

_____ 5. A chemical process in which a double sugar splits into two simple sugars.

B. SHORT ANSWER QUESTIONS

1. Using numbered steps, describe the procedure for boiling sugar to make pulled sugar.

2. Two major factors that affect the hardness of a finished pulled sugar piece are

   (a) _____.

   (b) _____.

3. Two precautions that should be observed in order to keep a boiling syrup from discoloring are

   (a) _____.

   (b) _____.

4. A simple mold that can be used to make sugar cages is a(n) _____.

5. To keep a sugar cage from sticking to the mold on which it is made, you should

_____.

6. In the space below, briefly describe how to make spun sugar.

7. Pulled sugar gets its name from the way it is manipulated. Describe how this is done.

_____

_____

_____.

This manipulation is done just until _____

_____.

8. If sugar is pulled too much, it will _____

_____.

9. While it is waiting to be shaped, pulled sugar is kept soft by _____

_____.